Ben

I CAN READ ABOUT

JULY 4TH, 1776

AMERICA'S FIRST BIRTHDAY

Written by Ellen Schultz

Illustrated by Herb Mott

Troll Associates

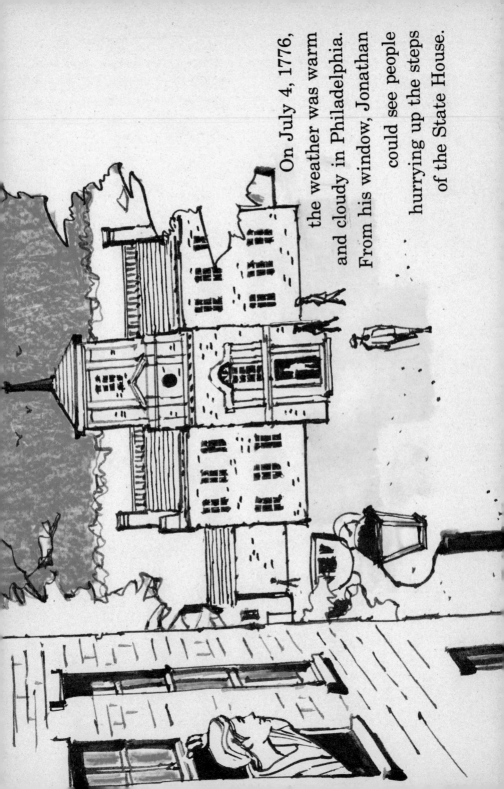

On July 4, 1776, the weather was warm and cloudy in Philadelphia. From his window, Jonathan could see people hurrying up the steps of the State House.

He knew that something important was about to happen— something that might change his life.

People were talking about *independence* for the thirteen colonies.

It was on everyone's mind.

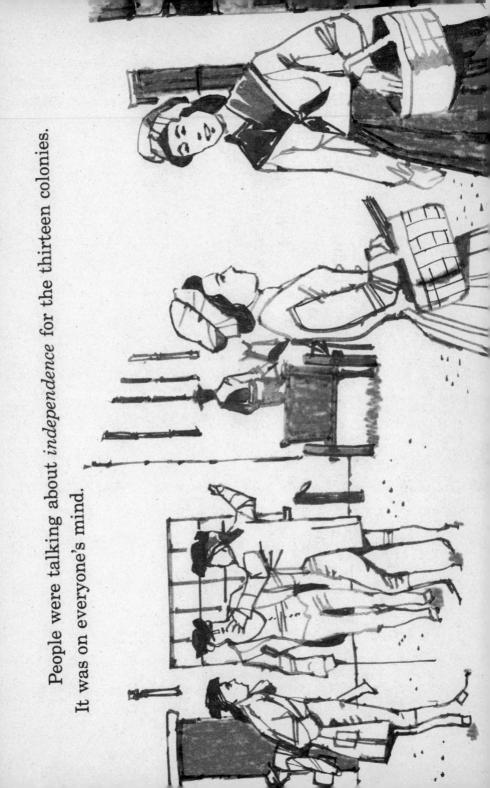

The *idea* of independence was not new in the thirteen colonies. Many people had come to the New World in search of freedom. One of the earliest groups were the Pilgrims, seeking religious freedom. They settled in Massachusetts and started a colony there.

Other settlers had started colonies in Virginia, the Carolinas, and Maryland.

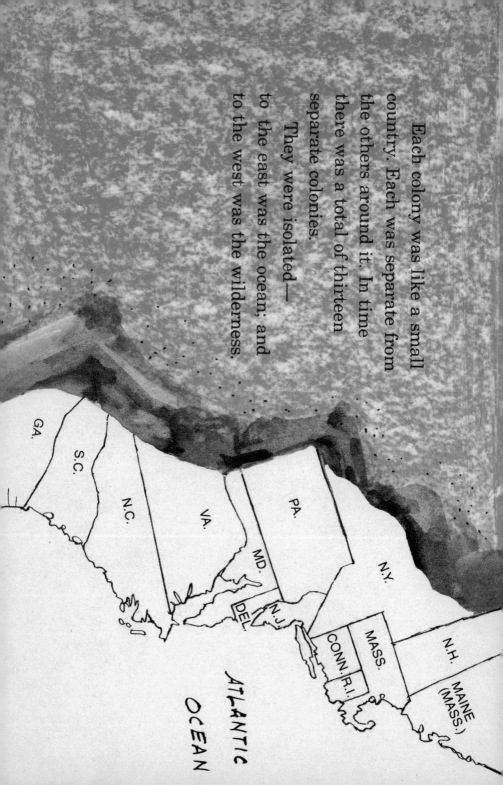

Each colony was like a small country. Each was separate from the others around it. In time there was a total of thirteen separate colonies.

They were isolated— to the east was the ocean; and to the west was the wilderness.

GA.

S.C.

N.C.

VA.

PA.

MD.

DEL.

N.J.

N.Y.

CONN. R.I.

MASS.

N.H.

MAINE (MASS.)

ATLANTIC OCEAN

Although people in towns were craftsmen and tradespeople, most Americans worked close to the land. They were farmers who grew what they needed to survive.

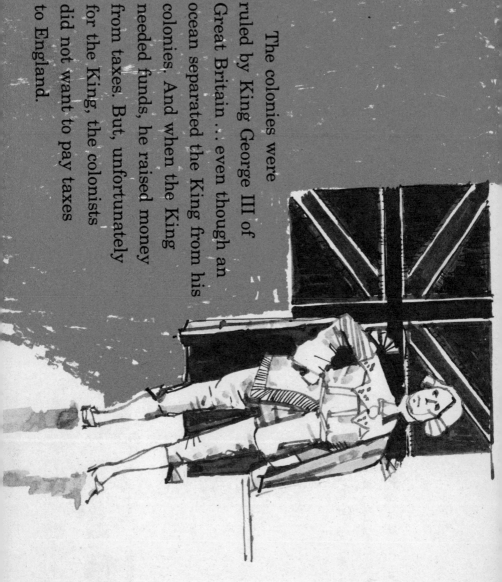

The colonies were
ruled by King George III of
Great Britain . . . even though an
ocean separated the King from his
colonies. And when the King
needed funds, he raised money
from taxes. But, unfortunately
for the King, the colonists
did not want to pay taxes
to England.

Jonathan's parents had told him about the Stamp Act of 1765. The colonists had to pay a tax on legal documents, newspapers, licenses and other important items. In 1767, taxes were put on paper, lead, paint, and tea.

The colonists complained. The parliament, or government of Britain, said it had the right to make all the laws for the colonies —on *any* matter. The colonists did not like being governed by a king who was thousands of miles away.

The colonies wanted more freedom but Great Britain was unwilling to give it to them.

Then, in 1773, a tax was put on tea coming into the colonies. The colonists were very angry over this tax on imported tea. How could they show their feelings?

One night in 1773, a group of colonists, dressed as Indians, climbed aboard the British ships in Boston Harbor and dumped all the tea overboard. The colonists would not pay the tax, nor would they drink the tea.

The King, of course, was very angry. Boston Harbor was closed down from shipping, and more British soldiers were sent to Massachusetts.

Fighting broke out as tension grew. Then, in 1775, the British learned that arms were being stored at Concord, Massachusetts. The British army marched from Boston to Concord. Along the way there was fighting at Lexington, and a battle at Concord. This was the start of the Revolutionary War between the colonies and Great Britain.

General George Washington was chosen to lead the troops. Farmers and blacksmiths and shopkeepers became soldiers overnight.

People now realized how important
it was for all thirteen colonies to
unite for their common cause.
No longer could they remain separate
and accomplish the same goals.
The time had come for the colonies
to stand together against the British.
It was time for *Independence*.

On May 10, 1775, delegates from the thirteen colonies gathered at the State House in Philadelphia to discuss the question of independence.

Their group was called the Second Continental Congress. Their ideas were so important that the delegates thought and debated among themselves for a year.

Finally, on June 7, 1776, the delegate from Virginia—Richard Henry Lee—proposed a course of action, or resolution, in Congress. "That these United Colonies are, and of right ought to be, free and independent States ..."

This important resolution to be free from Great Britain was not passed at once. The delegates talked among themselves. Who would present the *reasons* for independence?

Three days later the Congress voted to name five people to write a Declaration of Independence . . . if the delegates accepted Lee's resolution.

They were Benjamin Franklin of Pennsylvania, John Adams of Massachusetts, Thomas Jefferson of Virginia, Robert Livingston of New York, and Roger Sherman of Connecticut.

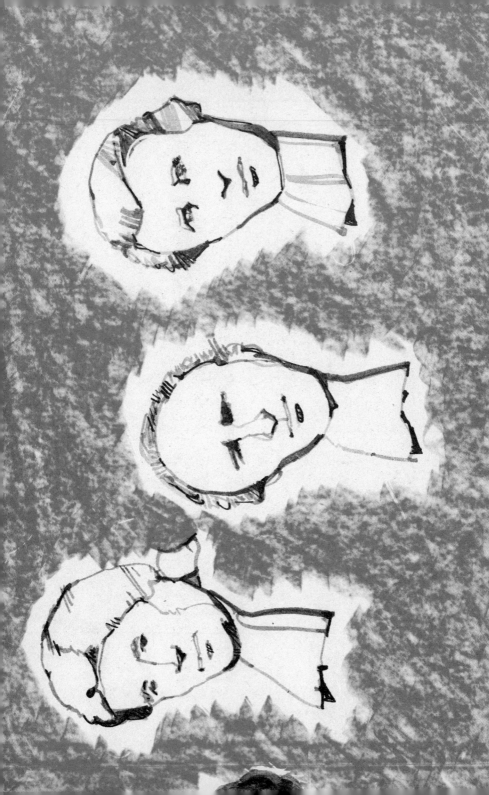

Thomas Jefferson was asked to do the actual writing of the Declaration because he was a skilled writer. The others, especially Franklin and Adams, would offer him guidance and advice.

Jefferson accepted the job, and finished the Declaration two weeks later.

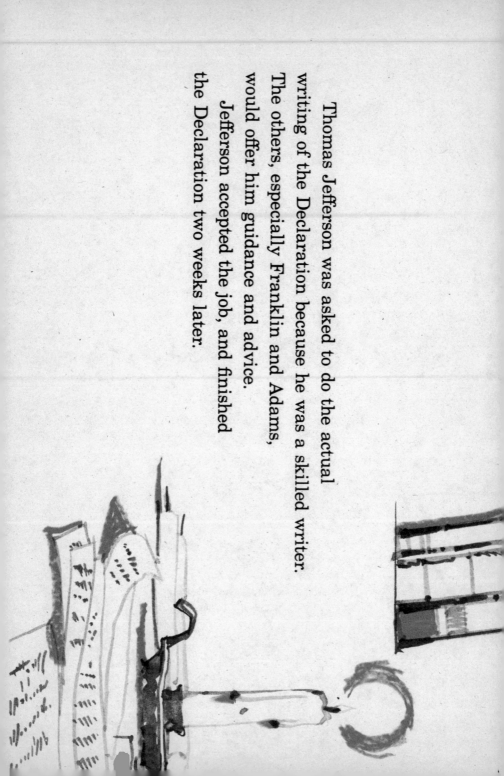

And now it was the fourth day of July in 1776, and the State House was aglow with activity. Perhaps this was the day everyone was waiting for.

The delegates from the thirteen colonies were about to vote on the most important issue of all—the Declaration of Independence.

Now it was up to the individual representatives of each colony to vote "Aye," or "Nay."

Would the Declaration pass? Would there be a new, independent nation today?

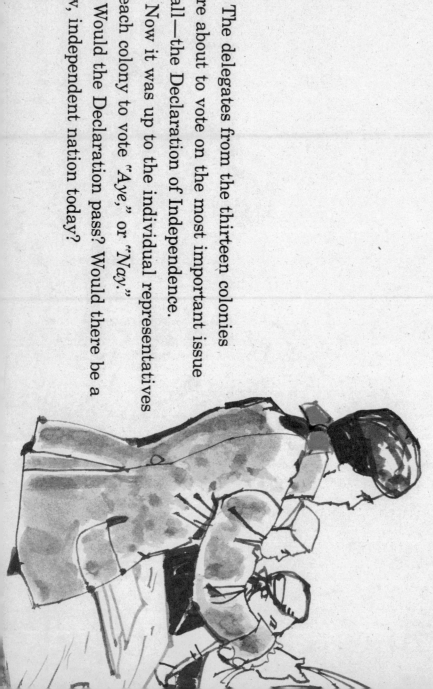

Late in the afternoon the Secretary of the Congress called for a vote. New York was not yet ready to cast a ballot, but the other twelve colonies voted one by one *for independence.*

And so it was done.

There was a moment of silence, because on this July 4, 1776, in the city of Philadelphia, a new, free, and independent nation had been born

—The United States of America.

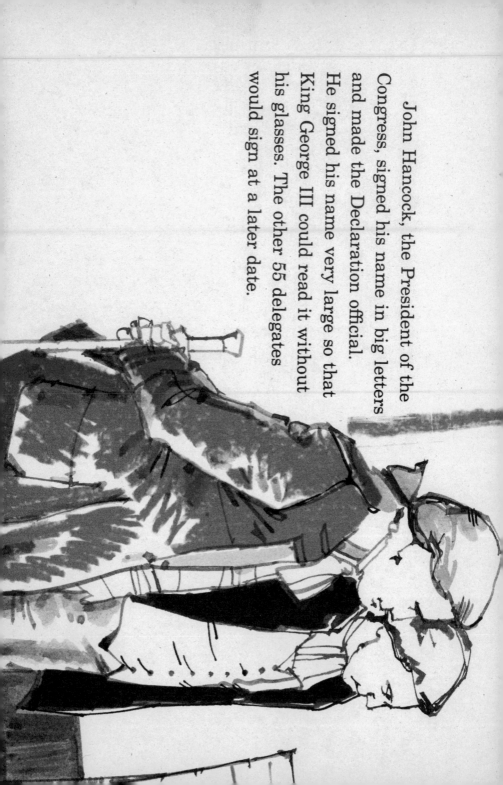

John Hancock, the President of the Congress, signed his name in big letters and made the Declaration official. He signed his name very large so that King George III could read it without his glasses. The other 55 delegates would sign at a later date.

Four days later on July 8th, bells called everyone to the State House courtyard. There the Declaration of Independence was read aloud for the first time, and Jonathan listened to the words.

Parts said "...that all men are created equal, that they are endowed with certain unalienable Rights, that among these are Life, Liberty and the pursuit of Happiness."

It also said that people had the right to choose their own form of government.

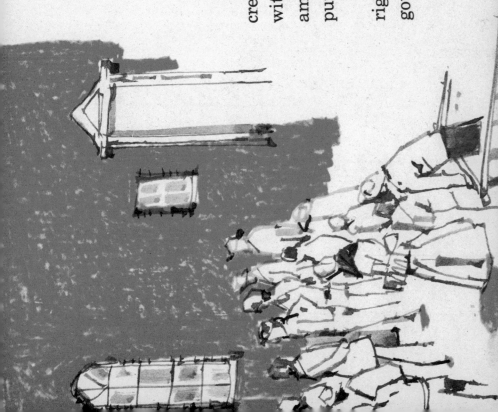

When it was finished, everyone cheered.
Bells rang. People made huge bonfires
and put candles in their windows.

Cannons were fired thirteen
times in honor of each new state.
Later there would be banquets. There
was joy and celebration everywhere . . .
even though the war was still ahead of them
and the new nation would have to win
its independence.

Jonathan raced through the streets with his friends. He was excited and proud. He was proud that he lived in the city of Philadelphia where all this had taken place. He was proud of the delegates who believed so strongly in freedom.

But most of all ... he was proud that as of July 4, 1776, he was a citizen of the *independent* United States of America.